Poets Diving in the Night

poems by

Nancy Dafoe

Finishing Line Press
Georgetown, Kentucky

Poets Diving in the Night

*For my brother Emerson, Jr.,
who dove into everything he did with passion
but lost his voice before losing his life*

Copyright © 2017 by Nancy Dafoe
ISBN 978-1-63534-104-1 First Edition
All rights reserved under International and Pan-American Copyright Conventions. No part of this book may be reproduced in any manner whatsoever without written permission from the publisher, except in the case of brief quotations embodied in critical articles and reviews.

ACKNOWLEDGMENTS

"Intertextual Lioness" was first published in the literary journal *The Ampersand, Vol. 4.*

"Lantern as Moon" first appeared in *The English Record*, journal of the New York State English Council, Winter 2014, Vol. 64, Number 1.

"From a Photograph of Children in Jean Lafitte National Park" won first place in the Soul Making Literary Competition in San Francisco.

"Returning to that Mineral State" first appeared in *An Iceberg in Paradise: A Passage through Alzheimer's,* published by SUNY Press in 2015.

"If you live near water" and "Abyssal Night" were finalists in the 2015 William Faulkner/ William Wisdom Creative Writing Competition.

    I would like to thank Leah Maines, Editor of Finishing Line Press, and my daughters Colette and Nicole Dafoe who read every poem multiple times, offered comments and encouragement. In addition, I extend my lasting gratitude to poets Gwynn O'Gara and Jo Pitkin for their support, commentary, and friendship.

Publisher: Leah Maines

Editor: Christen Kincaid

Cover Art: Photo of the Tomb of the Diver was taken by the author in Paestum, Italy. The ancient Greek image dates to approximately 470 B.C. and was discovered beneath the ruins of the Italian city. The wall in the picture represents the known world from which the diver is leaving.

Author Photo: Parker Stone II Photography

Cover Design: Elizabeth Maines

Printed in the USA on acid-free paper.
Order online: www.finishinglinepress.com
          also available on amazon.com

          Author inquiries and mail orders:
                Finishing Line Press
                  P. O. Box 1626
            Georgetown, Kentucky 40324
                    U. S. A.

Table of Contents

Corporeal Ghost 1

Intertextual Lioness 2

Abyssal night 4

Lines composed on the shores of Lac Yser 5

Lantern as Moon 6

Things the Water Carried 8

From a Photograph of Children in Jean Lafitte
    National Park 9

Fourteen Ways of Looking at a Pelican 11

Female Principles 13

Marie Colvin in "The Waste Land" 14

Fate 16

Waking as Darwin 18

Running Interference 19

Joining Calvino's Baron in the Trees 22

High Tension 24

Heartbreak of You 25

Bird: Equivalent of Revelation 26

If you live near water 29

What is this Mecca? 30

Returning to that Mineral State 31

Language like Water 33

*This paradox—this intermittently maddening and
divine plunge into all that lies below language—
using language,
is for all divers in the night.*

Corporeal Ghost

Shimmering far below surface
  water-worn features
     swimming out of long ago frozen gullies, leaving visible trace:
          carbonate imprints on rock until rains
              coursed down,
                    down

      where our lungs are aching,
            eardrums bleeding,
   saw-edged spine nearly invisible as it circles round,
   shape neither angel nor devil, its wings floating
on invisible current   that swells—   embraces
    as albino Manta assumes semblance
                of God's messenger
                at the
  periphery:

              aqueous
              luminous
                kite

Intertextual Lioness

For me, it was the arthritic lioness
at the National Zoo, neither Ted Hughes'
nor Amy Lowell's pike, not Mark Doty's
Display of Mackerel nor Yeats' Swan,
not even William Carlos Williams'
sparrow perched by his window;
neither Robert Lowell's procession
of little skunks, nor Elizabeth Bishop's armadillo,
my imprinted lioness of advanced age,
with camel-like seroma between
her shoulder blades, was closer
to Blake's "*Tyger! burning bright*,"
more akin to Pablo Neruda's puma
with "*alcoholic eyes.*"
But while on the subject of beasts,
this lioness was hardly Diane Ackerman's
"*Jaguar of sweet laughter,*"
certainly not D.H. Lawrence's
Elephants "*slow to mate,*"
not the hippopotamus of an erudite Eliot,
this lioness suddenly older than time:
transcendent,
her stare as intimate as Annie Dillard's
close encounter with a weasel.
This grand old dame no longer a queen,
whose Prince Hamlet, in separate
but adjacent enclosure, had rejected her
long ago.
Their juxtaposition
could not be more pronounced.

Lioness here no griffin, no stone Gargoyle;
she was as earthbound as me,
surveying the Zoo crowd
with neither contempt nor passion,
her opaque skills as huntress as unimaginable
as Africa from this vantage point.

But it was not the fabulous mane of lion
who haunted me long after leaving
to fight traffic.

When I think of it again,
perhaps that rough-haired female cat,
walking with a stroke victim's gait,
her squinting eyes and grimacing, wrinkled face,
wearing wisdom and disdain,
was yet like Roethke's swan,
whose low, rumbling sighs spoke
of a "*Socrates of snow.*"
This lioness was, it turns out, as lyrical
as William Carlos Williams' sparrow,
that same sparrow chirping "*poetic truth*"
in late afternoon, altered light.

Abyssal night

We've been living with Hamlet for a while now,
stalled at his final syllables because, really,
where can any of us go from there?
                              "The rest is silence"
slipping beneath surface in cadence,
through crevice, along with Nathalie Sarraute,
we question, what takes place below language?
Articulation not the point at all
but, rather, manifestation of inaction,
sorrow, and naturally or unnaturally death,
and we realize without intending,
that we, too, have been collecting in the midst
of trying to bring home Beckett's unwilling Godot
who has kept us all waiting   …   all these years.

Even before these sudden arrivals
at 10:00 at night when we weren't expecting
company, Mrs. Dalloway suggested with a glance
at fluttering curtains mimicking flutter in her heart
that we should have known from absence
of Jacob's voice in Jacob's Room
because we don't so much know
boy or man as come to apprehend loss.
Sartre intimating Faulkner's shadows
streaming, "like an underground river"

Why these "Tropisms" around silence?
How maddening for writers to discover
it is not at all about orientation
in Nemerov's symbolic motel room
or linguistic acrobatics; it is not even attached
to signature ellipsis portending more to come…
We're *Here*, Sarraute's *Here* again,
laying down narrative, synecdoche,
whispers and howls:
chiseling stone in darkness.

Lines composed on the shores of Lac Yser

In which the heavy and the weary weight
Of all this unintelligible world,
Is lightened
William Wordsworth,
Lines Composed a Few Miles above Tintern Abbey

Between charcoaled tree line and dense storm clouds,
sliver of whitish blue suggests darkness will break.
Canadian tiger swallowtails flittering;
transformation met by wind blowing back and black
demarcations mimicking stripes on birch and aspen.

Nervous American black duck emerges from the forest,
her feathers glisten with caught water; she shakes, dropping light.
With her ducklings dabbling in shallows,
she stretches, her speculum revealing brilliant blue.

Ghost flights across silver bow of aluminum boat,
lambent, casting golden irregular lines
like sunlight on river rock.

Light, dark paradox everywhere—
even the underside of closed eyelids:

imprint where light is swallowed in eclipse.

Lantern as Moon

Concealed by cryptic memory,
scene opens slowly with a lantern as moon
guiding my way down steep banks
to black river in the icy cold
of early spring, breaths frosty, limbs excited
as we scampered over rocks leading
to water's edge, holding out light
that caught fish flashing,
our dip nets yawning and anxious
to scoop mouthfuls of rainbow smelt
into white pails: catch of the luminous
during this middle of the night run,
temperature again plummeting,
creek swollen with brilliance;
father and grandfather ventured out boldly
in hip-waders as my bothers leaned over rocks,
peering into frenzy of aphotic waters.

When father re-emerged, he held a living net
that spoke of rivers, earth, and powerful oils.
Brothers slipping their fingers into buckets
and laughing at the way fish wiggled
from their grasp, plunging both hands
into the mix to hold slippery scales;
I had forgotten wearing father's watch.
Pulling out in a panic, I dried the time piece,
but realized no one saw my slip and dove
back into numbing cold. Water itself alive.

On the banks along and above the bridge
were fishermen, but night was still;
absoluteness of dark, punctuated
only by narrow beams of lantern light,
insulating us into communities, hushed
by sudden, unexpected bounty.

Mother was waiting at my grandparents'
patchwork-shingled house with a baby
in her arms. She never went on those night-time
foraging expeditions but was always relieved
when we returned safely, cold and "talking
a-mile-a-minute." It was only later that I thought
about how hard it must have been for my grandmother
to have our sprawling family descend upon her home
with its empty larder. Although Father cut heads
off little fishes, spreading old newspapers
over the table, as we gathered around—
recoiling slightly at the sight—it was Mother
who floured and fried fish. I held my baby sister
while the women lopped off chunks of lard
to ladle into cast iron popping with the dance.
Fed with chunks of wood, beast of a ravenous stove
heated the kitchen until we had forgotten our chill.

I don't remember being hungry as a child,
but we were excited by the prospect of food.
I never thought about my grandfather's job as a tanner
in a shoe factory where his lungs were slowly coated
in a process to prevent putrefaction. He was to die
a few years later. I had no idea at the time
of the fears of the adults around me,
only that it all seemed part of an adventure.
We stayed up late, limits blown out, and ate
sweet, fresh fish, rare in the days when no one
had money but didn't know they were poor.

Until I woke one morning realizing the dream
was a distant memory and the memory a dream
of discovery in which my father, mother, brother,
and grandparents, now long gone, emerge
vividly luminous—first concealed then illuminated
by swings of a false moon.

Things the Water Carried

Long after your eye has released them,
the mind holds onto jagged lines,
producing that split suggested by Descartes
as he built bridges across an impossible gap
you recognize today as philosophy
and neuroscience entering your cabin.

States altered everywhere as light
and dark exchange places by peregrination.
Thunder—silencing even insects
and birds momentarily—a conversation
held in the distance between old gods,
as Plato's Forms: unexpected guests.

Even restless feet of a mouse pause
in creature's wonder, terror, or awe
you can only empathize with while you watch
a light show in dark: juxtaposition of antipodes
working as waves are whipped to frenzy,
frothing at indistinct shorelines.

At the end of the storm, you venture
outside, walk the beach to find
bloated carp arrived upside down,
plastic bag breathing in sunlight, whitened,
barkless tree limb resembling slender arm,
Styrofoam container gleaming,

its white skin wrapped by red rope
attached to matted, gray bird missing
one eye: struggle between natural world
and one we've manufactured.
Over the tops of mountains, the rumble widens,
vibration not of thunder but distant airplane.

From a Photograph of Children in Jean Lafitte National Park

All those years ago, we walked
to the National Cemetery in Chalmette
where we lingered among the weathered crypts,
discolored bricks, showing through cement glaze
that was slowly breaking down grays,
black mildew adorning stone
like painted inflections. I noted surprising
color in figurines of the Virgin Mary
in cryptic enclosures within headstones,
iron lace of railings and wrought-iron chairs showing
beautiful decay haunting us as we wandered
to the pirate's National Park, Jean Lafitte honored
for coming to aid of a racist General Jackson
all those years ago. Between land and water—
always water—between Decatur and Canal Streets,
between the Mississippi and Lake Pontchartrain,
we came upon a group of children.

I was photographing the canal
when they ran onto the stone bridge and waved,
their multicolored coats creating a rainbow
reflected in water. Waving back,
I took their picture before walking
to a grove of trees spun with delicate moss,
the children catching up to me, laughing
and running. They stood before me,
tightly together; unaware of wide angle lens,
they smiled, knowing I would again photograph
them, this time close up, their beautiful black faces
articulated on black and white film.

It was only later, when I had developed
all the photographs in my darkroom in New York
that I was struck by their divine grace,
this toned print revealing exhilarant optimism
even as their brightly colored coats were transposed
in shades of gray.
I would come back to this portrait
again and again, struck by these seraphim,
as well as photographic composition
when news of Hurricane Katrina's wrath
blew through.

Focusing on their sweet faces,
I feared for them, wondering
how those eight-year-olds—now eighteen—
had come through storm, infested waters,
and slow political embroilment, resulting
in unheeded cries for help. Thinking
of them as I recalled images of corpses floating,
the push and shove for a seat on a bus out
of New Orleans: trepidation in the eyes
of citizens of a city built
between waters and dreams.

Fourteen Ways of Looking at a Pelican

Scanning the horizon, three flew into view:
beginning on a slant line, yet nothing appeared ontological,
looking at these indelicate pelicans

until distraction fell away to signifier, uniting thoughts,
Dante leading with a line from *Paradiso*, recalling
and symbolizing Christ as "Nostro Pelicano"

Trinity's resonance leveled at sight line: paradox
of comedic yet graceful flight of this top heavy bird,
arc foiled by too long a bloodied bill

Unpredictable yet cosmic order found in interpretation
of a man in a woman in a pelican symbolization
in which bird is both Christ and mother to her young

Christian iconography embraced from an older time:
sincere mother bird wounding herself to feed starving young;
allegorical pelican in her piety: "repast them" with her blood

Gular pouch storing for later contemplation;
ancient Egyptians referred to Pelican as "Mother of the King,"
proposing she offered passage of the living to the dead

Linked to the Philosopher Stone through speculation,
bird a conceptualization of soul development—
this unlikely spiritual messenger.

Brown bird mirroring mystery, diving beneath
water's surface just as poets enter amalgam of language,
searching for evocative perfection

Pelican's bill is abundance, like line in a book: sentence
carried away by its author too in love with language
to stop, yet punctuated with a hook

Level flight lines low over Gulf waters:
one bird followed by another completing the line,
suggesting more than syntax

Transformative bard Shakespeare acknowledged
debt in his lines from *Hamlet* and *King Lear*,
pointing a finger at those "Pelican daughters"

Darwin would have marveled at the stability
of their 30-million-year old flight;
fossil record scarcely changed by evolution

Wallace Stevens first wrote *Thirteen Ways of Looking
at a Blackbird*, but the pelican's eye knows more of *innuendos*
and *inflections* than even the eye of a blackbird, this pelican

imbued with our long, dangerous history
of recorded thought: Greeks naming her *pelekan*,
flying in enigmatically from *pelekys*—axe

Female Principles

How is it women came to be metonymically
represented as soul while men call up body or mind?
She wonders, closing a book on Plato
before falling asleep, chin still resting
in soft palm of her hand; she dreams
with an eye partially open, half alert,
hearing crystals break against glass panes;
only then, when she is up
and looking out into blue blackness,
does grousing dog
slightly rouse himself, growl indiscriminately,
then nod lazily at nonexistent
intruder, extending his slumber,
cat already padding softly,
warily through jungles
of her velvet rooms.

Marie Colvin in "The Waste Land"

"*Here is the one-eyed*" journalist,
Marie's left—patched like a pirate's—
a casualty of mortar fire and establishing fact—
carefully extracted from ruins:
splintered bone and blood-filled shoes,
her own in a hall that last night:
details of lives drawn from dry wells,
in this smoldering desert light,
in which Conrad captured his comrade
in last image—her back to camera,
slender fingers still holding her pen
to dash off reports on a pad pressed
against metal grating: composition
once a kitchen where a window
had been. This is most telling:
Marie stands with the heel of her boot
balanced on mounds of war,
scrap and dust beneath her foot
as she writes about children and death
in a hole hollowed by shelling.

T.S. Eliot once exhorted,
"Marie, Marie, hold on tight," and Marie
held on for as long as she could, denying
surrender, past open graves, past rational fears.
February was already a cruel month
long before it became the month
Marie Colvin lost her life
under rubble of a building in Homs.

Libya, Chechnya, Kosovo,
these lands of ancient to contemporary strife,
Sierra Leone, Zimbabwe, Sri Lanka, East Timor,
Syria, the last where she asked
questions many were unwilling to,
or were we unaware of these places

of inverted towers?
But Marie was not like most,
this clear-eyed journalist
who chose war zones
for telling truths about atrocities done
to women and children, to innocents
and innocence in the middle of the night.
Not some distant, faceless objects,
these lands and peoples were real
and individual to Marie and to us perhaps
because she chose first and never needed
to ask, "What have I given?"

With only one good eye, Marie saw
and foresaw the rest. Her eye never failed
her even when her written words ceased
to fill another desert with unassailable voice.

Fate

They did everything right;
elaborately designed, articulated:
"Human Chandelier" balanced
not on the head of a pin
but on fate constructed on metal frame—
intricate, failsafe—eight women
head-to-head, 35 feet up in the air.
Holding on by their hair,
they held no sway nor indecision,
neither tempted by applause below
nor moved by nearly imperceptible voices above:
all concentration. Their communion an aerial,
performed dozens of times,
suspended from rigging by human hair.

We've done nothing wrong, they said.
"*Heads, Heads, Heads, Heads,*" so begins
Rosencrantz and Guildenstern are Dead.
"Who decides? *Decides? It is written.*"
The play on words in a play,
Tom Stoppard's take on fate.

When a clamp, a clip, snapped—
their beautiful bodies plunged,
not the embodiment but their actual bodies,
their fall inescapable
as timing, phrasing.
Signs of sisters holding sisters like poetry
by the thinnest of threads.

They, too, were tumblers,
all of us spectators to spectacle,
but this time, just this once—
it lands on Heads. They fell not to their deaths,
broken,
> yet
> still
> tumbling—
recursive not regressive—
these wondrous women fell not into deaths
but back into their lives.

Waking as Darwin

Pounding jars teeth, unsettles jaw;
boat slaps waves that curl and split;
in the distance, coins glint at crests before falling.
All the while, you search for something.

Imagine waking as Darwin—to sunscape in Galapagos,
to sighing sounds of breakers, rushing sea
                    through islets,
you, walking carefully so as not to twist an ankle
on lava-formed rocks—pitted, craterous surface
digging into your palm as you settle into position;
salted lichen crushed with each adjustment.

You take out a notebook and set it on your lap
as your brined hand feels both heat and ancient ridges
of tortoise shell, patterns written in brain's creases
where you're counting, recording
because you're Darwin and understand
that these details will be important;
one of the finches flutters then perches,
pecking at seedlings, chirping its warble
then harsh, descending notes,
seeming to know your discovery depends
on slight hook, size, and shape of its beak,
and you observe with breaths
of an urgent wind its differences
from specimens you saw last week
on Charles, now Floreana.

When you wake,
they shout, deny—
like some ancient, historical Judas—
your careful science,
our evolution.

Running Interference

                I
I might have noticed bright red
wings or pointed crest
like a remark, if he had not
tried to murder his own image
like some madman,
wings thumping against unforgiving
glass repeatedly; all summer long
he kept at it. How he recovered
his senses I'll never know,
having seen birds dive
into windows and break
their fragile necks. Unwilling
to watch it continue, I placed
broom, bristles up and facing out,
against double panes,
against uncertain reflections,
but he shook feathered appendages
in paroxysms of small fury,
throttling his doppelganger
with resilience and rhythm
of a blacksmith at his wrought irons
or more like Lowell
on a terrible, dark night
before he witnessed
a family of skunks.
Then I turned on lights, altering space,
this boundary of crossed handles—
a mop and a maze of objects broke the spell,
releasing the cardinal.

II

Along the Seneca River,
a man came across a hawk
ensnared in line strung like spider silk
over a river, tangling talons
of trapped assassin, twisting around
and around until great red tail
flew upside down, surveying futility
with wild wings. What drew man
was not hawk wrestling air
but a murder of crows descending.

Mortal enemies with roles
reversed, the crows dove and pecked
at raptor that swung furiously
from its impossible perch.
Man on the bank scooped snow
into his gloveless hands
and threw ice balls one after another
at specimens of the genus Corvus
until his shoulders ached, his back
cramped, his fingers grew numb
and red, those hands he used
to fight descending black birds
while hunter hung perilously,
crows like mad dogs barking
at the interference of human
who would not give up on hawk,
hour passing hour.

What prime directive?
No non-interference clause
when we have already tipped
every balance, he reasons.
When, as suddenly as it began,
invisible filaments snap in tension,
releasing those wide, imposing wings
in free fall until Buteo Jamaicensis
finds again the familiar in descent,
crows rapidly dispersing,
the man on the bank turning away,
while hawk soars
late into morning.

Joining Calvino's Baron in the Trees

I

High in an ancient, virgin Ilex with its vast
baldachin, a cicada flexes its tender timbrels
while the leathery, evergreen leaves parallel
dry ground that runs down toward the past.
From up in the canopy, you may cast
your lofty gaze down to ancient citadel
of Santa Marie di Castellabate's jewels
that punctuate the coast with its cast
of Terra Cotta tiles baking in earth's fire clay
oven above operatic coloratura of rich
ochres in golds and alabasters that enrich
a painter's dreams. Italy is a rare cache
of wonders that mark the bewitched
Michelangelo's or Leonardo's fevered pitch.

II

In contrast to her hamlets, the sea swell
shimmers, blending in an absent horizon
at dusk and dawn until winds and sun emblazon
the once indistinguishable again as part of spell
of waters that turn deeper blue than sky, then propel
white sails on the Tyrrhenian against horizon,
leaving its pearly and vanishing trail as you gaze on
then follow the lonely, curving lines that compel
a painter's eye up the side of elevation
in scarring, angular strokes up to the *comune*
of Castellabate, the township seemingly immune
to raiding pirates. With its castle, location
signaled by abbot's fortress but also marooned:
invitation to conquerors, isolation opportune.

III

Venerable ilex at once separating you and Italo
Calvino's Baron—who took to branches of trees—
the rest of humanity seen from a makeshift trapeze.
While festival drummers beat far below,
fisherman whistle, the wash hung in tableau:
breaking glass, a beggar pockets coins then flees,
muffled noise of barking dogs answer braying donkeys.
Yet paradoxically, ilex also connects you to the flow

through its intricate tangle of roots, threaded out
over hillsides. You observe from trees an intense
sound of lonely cicada that disturbs you to such extent
that you mistake the Baron's demeanor for doubt.
He gently reminds you of harsh cicada's defense:
symbol of antipodes of rebirth and evanescence.

High Tension

Poet's voice was tremulous, inexperienced,
childlike, as if words spoken at the reading
were her first audible syllables. Her voice chirping
then gliding until she reached a rich vibrato.

She had lost her voice entirely once,
not figuratively, she informed us,
but literally, her vocal chords paralyzed—
although she never stopped writing and rewriting,
perfecting a poem twenty years
in the making. For some time, after losing
her voice, she experienced audio illusion,
reliving that sorrow, distinctly remembering
her hidden sounds as she formed
shapes of vowels and consonants
in their latency, fingerprints left behind
at the scene of high tension.

Just when she had given up hope
of ever speaking her own utterances
existing years in dormancy,
she spoke, surprising her new husband
with the sweetness and cadence
of vocalization, struck nearly dumb
again at actuality of hearing discourse roll
over her tongue, tickle her lips, and resonate
in full throat. All the while,
written words had sustained her,
given promise, liberating her soul
from biology.

Poem narrates girl with disappearing song
still traceable in echo when the poet finished
in frail strand suggestive of instrument's frustration,
sorrow, and, on the eve of her reading, ascendency.

Heartbreak of You

Dear boy,
You are 32 and look 19, charming and smart, with impish
"I did something slightly wrong" sort of smile,
that dimple a relic from another age.

"I am nothing," you whisper hoarsely, "nothing more than wind,"
incessant force pushing past doorways, through windows,
blowing out closed ones.

You surrender to long drawn breath,
poison arrow in your arm. Yelp and whoosh, it seems,
of expectant company, but wind is its own companion:
multi-layered voice of aloneness, this wounding wind of you.
Howling upon entering, wind leaves space between walls
trembling, naked but unafraid, your invading wind
not sparing grief's ever-lengthening shadow.

This wind you have become is lost lover blinded
by debris washed in blind eyes, this wind of consequence
blowing color from our faces, striking like the hurricane
you imagine yourself to be, arriving like the flood
you precipitate. As suddenly as doors are loosened
and curtains disappeared from gaping holes once glazed,
your shell of a house is gone;
rains sweeping in, weeping down walls,
over your long journey from disappointment and sadness
to hollowed-out frame; this hot wind blowing
through your too big heart until your rooms and hallways
are emptied and you slump, envenomed thorn inside you,
clarifying nothing.

Yet you have become wind:
no longer hollow but hallowed.

Bird: Equivalent of Revelation

A blue heron extends its neck,
beak and head equipoised
like a spring uncoiled,
serpentining with each step,
lunging forward,
as it deliberately stalks,
not gracefully, along the
ragged shoreline
in front of my window.
Taken to flight, this bird
seems prehistoric and
startlingly eminent.

On land, it is awkward, archaic,
a living, feathered fossil
that moves me to meditate
on the Avian Influenza A
carried in birds, a virus
crossing over, transcendent,
as it reaches from birds to
humans, an evolving pandemic:

a Vietnamese man photographed
kissing the broken neck of his
prized rooster killed in a cockfight,
the man later captured by the
photographer in death throes
as his lungs collapse from
the weight of an invading army,
a bird the offender even when
sacrificial,
calling forth an image—

of my sister trapped
in a blood-spattered house
with flying gore, the child
slipping on a clot,
as a disoriented starling
darted blindly, and the girl ran
screaming, finally hiding before
I could arrive to save her,
and she suffers from
this gruesome intimacy.

"To this day," she states,
"I hate birds." That starling's neck
broken against a pane of glass,
causing me to reflect
on a rush of wings,

as Dillard writes,
"A sound of beaten air,
like a million shook rugs,"
her Pilgrim, an unwilling
witness to the roosting starlings
that have gathered in the tree
outside my bedroom,
assembling this congress
of fanaticism, making it impossible
to sleep, so I am already
at the window when
they soar in some
single,
terrible
volition,

reminding me of a terrorist
with a pack of explosives,
strapped to his chest,
arriving at zealotry
from resignation to the aggregate
in a paroxysm of fury,
taking flight in annihilation,
grief raining down on the innocent
and the guilty alike as

this convocation of rooks cast
a shadow overhead,
their aerodynamics the
stimulus of revelation:
da Vinci pursuing
the architecture of
flight as we ascend
on an assemblage
of words fluttering
across a page.

If you live near water

If you live near water,
you will see ripples catching light
moving across a line of trees like piano keys
played: a scale recording
birds cackling, cawing, chirping,
screeching or cooing in early morning
with such urgency that you wake
to enter their conversations,
acknowledge after emergence
from sleep the calming effect
of wide vistas,
only occasionally disturbed by craft,
but you also observe
gathering masses of detached seaweed
floating like dirty carpets, slime algae
protruding above agitated surface like boils
on infected skin; dock aged and splintering,
feathers of an unfortunate bird bobbing
like tiny white boats too delicate to survive long,
a mayfly adult reaching the end
of abbreviated life, floating on tension
between water and air, crippled
and struggling, its motions inadvertent call
to minnows below, birds above.

After composing lines or casting a line,
you look up to notice a spider has strung
its thread from raft to cloth shirt
covering your arm, attaching
as the order of arachnids does without
slightest concern for longevity;
evocation of temporality, fate, fear,
and variously hope or hopelessness—
something elementally human.

What is this Mecca,

this Jerusalem, this Temple,
this Basilica that morphs in shape and size,
extending beyond our apparent comprehension?

Beyond lanky sea grass that bends
with a ballerina's agonized grace,
pilgrims wind their way over dunes,
stopping momentarily, silenced.
Sand gives way repeatedly,
making entrance arduous going
until grains congeal wet and jeweled,
a footprint indelible only fleetingly
before each swell rushes in to claim it.

Women with short-cropped hair,
their spines no longer straight, begin a journey
at an indistinct line where the sun's glint
on the sea tempts with apocryphal pathway
as if offering a crossing like Christ's across
tranquility, but swells rise up further out,
distending from older forces as a lone
jogger runs parallel to movable line of shore
and sea, navigating an irregular course.

A father and his young sons
chase an Irish setter into the surf, splashing,
tumbling, as a football soars between
them, falling to earth with gravity
then floating in swells. An elderly couple
teeter in the too-soft footing up ahead,
as a solitary writer, without a notebook,
collects evidence, following disappearing
print of a man's sneaker, a child's bare foot,
the
paw
mark
of
a
dog.

Returning to that Mineral State

I

Something about a stone, a stone,
a stone—when my nephew placed
little colored rocks on marbled
gravestone that marked where
my brother lay, it wasn't a tradition
I knew, but one that was comforting,
so I continued to bring him white
quartz and red-veined granite
from shores near our cabin, where
I found myself searching for stones
then thinking of the past as we kids
smashed shale slabs, peering inside
mysteries, and we pressed fingers
into indentations,
feeling ridges left by shells
harboring ancient lives, and it seemed,
when I was young,
that a stone could talk.

II

Carrying a smooth, black pebble
for luck, I rubbed it long, remembering
my brother watching me skimming
a stone across surface, breaking tension.

III

I find I fit inside a W.S. Merwin stone
poem, recognizing Beckett and Shakespeare
and Kenyon who in her power gave us
a stone, and Wilfred Wilson Gibson who
sought out stones, and Margo Berdeshevsky
whose book *Between Soul and Stone*
resides in this dense, layered abode.
Turning it over and over in my palm
—this stone that could take our worry,
mark our dead,
record our time—
slips and skips
across calm waters,
and I watch until all that is shown
is a stone, a stone, a stone.

Language like Water

Drip drop
conduit: vowel   owl
flying   floating   to surface
string of syllables rippling in ear's canal,
consonants descending to depths
language unbound from strictures of grammar
but not syntax, arranged atom by atom
molecules attaching as letters—signifier,
signified until there is some semblance

Everything sounds like water:
cars rushing, leaves attached to trees, fans whirring;
creatures swimming, drinking, drowning;
Danielle Vogel's "Between Grammars" with parentheses
gulping because there is no air beneath this surface;
bathing then diving, words displaced:
the way back restricted,
undercurrents in our blood transporting
without directive, language turning and turning
serous like Yeats' "widening gyre,"
we whirl; words falling, splashing, crashing
with force enough to sculpt rock we can read

Breathe in harbors of coral language
and sunken shipwrecked letters;
waterfalls in water, of water, under water
orbiting arc through water gardens

To the west of Mariana Islands,
life where no life should exist,
plates mapped out; lakes inside an ocean
exist as science not magic realism;
words lacustrine, new growth as geological strata,
this language eupotamic,
thriving where none should be;
water defying paltry attempts to make streets

aqueous false boundaries
at limits of backrush;
littoral drift under the influence
angle of incidence scarp,
calving at poles of antithesis;
motion at the bottom caused by density;
words jumbled, carried further from source

Estuaries,
submerged sounds in incoherence
until born in water again and again,
yet again forgetting origins

Writing of the sea,
myth diving in anticipation;
reading ripples, deciphering codes—
sounds of breathing
No litany of poets, but we find them at water's edge

Here quiet water ripples, caught by reeds,
insects skim on summer skates;
dragonflies mate on surface tension,
an angler's flotilla

What is this language of water,
of lakes, seas, rivers, streams?

We hold conch to our ears and imagine
we hear her voice in that enameled chamber

Perhaps we become vessels sailing, gliding
over waters until storms come;
then we are overturned,
fall into drowning, panicking, losing our way
until remembering our beginning:
language of incoherence
and discovery

Poet, writer, and educator **Nancy Avery Dafoe** has published books on teaching writing: *Breaking Open the Box* and *Writing Creatively: A Guided Journal* through Rowman & Littlefield Education in 2013 and 2014, respectively. Her latest book on education, *The Misdirection of Education Policy: Raising Questions about School Reform*, was released from publisher Rowman & Littlefield in June 2016. Her cross-genre memoir and poetry book, *An Iceberg in Paradise: A Passage through Alzheimer's*, was published by SUNY Press in 2015.

Dafoe's poems, essays, and stories have appeared in numerous literary publications and won awards locally and nationally. Her fiction work also appears in the anthology *Lost Orchard*, published by SUNY Press in 2014. She won the William Faulkner/William Wisdom poetry prize in 2016.

After working in high school as an AP English Literature and Composition, journalism, and college prep English teacher, as well as in a community college as an adjunct instructor, Dafoe retired from full-time teaching to write and do consulting work through Dafoe Writing & Consulting. A member of the Central New York Branch of the National League of American Pen Women (NLAPW), she currently offers writing courses and editorial services through her website www.dafoewritingandconsulting.com.

She lives in Homer, New York with her husband Daniel and son Blaise. She has two daughters, Colette and Nicole, and three grandsons, Truman, Owen, and Enzo.

www.ingramcontent.com/pod-product-compliance
Lightning Source LLC
LaVergne TN
LVHW041603070426
835507LV00011B/1274